Think On These Things For Men

Quotes, Bible Verses, and affirmations

Felice S.C

For more information, kindly email the author at rightsideceo@yahoo.com
feliciacauley@ymail.com. www.rightsidepiblishing.com

Published by Right Side Publishing
Print in the United States
Project manager Robert Cauley
Editor: Felicia S. Cauley
Cover design by Tiny Rhodes
Interior Design by Felicia S Cauley

Think On These Things For Men

Quotes, Bible Verses, and affirmations

Felice S. C

Table of Contents

Felice S.C

This book is Dedicated to My Husband

Robert A.Cauley

Son John W Willis Jr.

And my brothers in Christ

John Banks

Keith Muse

&

Brandon Mitchell

Acknowledgments

SPECIAL THANKS TO:

Solomon Moses and my friends from Nigeria, I could not have put this book together without your dedication and research on the needs and issues men are faced with.

Men are essential and are capable of being good leaders, sons, husbands, and role models if they are given the proper tools to use in their everyday life.

May God give you the strength and the courage to lead your family under the authority of Jesus Christ who is a good father.

A man is a provider

Godly men provide for their families

1 Timothy 5:8 But if any provide not for his own, and especially for those of his own house, he hath denied the faith, and is worse than an infidel.

Focus on the things of God

Do not pursue the things of the world
Instead, pursue the things of God

1 Timothy 6:11 - But thou, O man of God, flee these things; and follow after righteousness, godliness, faith, love, patience, meekness.

The example to follow

Set your standards high. No standard is higher than the example of Christ.

1 Peter 1:15-16 But as he which hath called you is holy, so be ye holy in all manner of conversation; Because it is written, Be ye holy; for I am holy.

Sexual Immorality

Pornography is not of God. It is sexually immoral. Be careful what you allow yourself to watch and consume.

1 Corinthians 6:18 Flee fornication. Every sin that a man doeth is without the body; but he that committeth fornication sinneth against his own body.

Mentorship Every Man needs a Mentor.

1 Peter 5:5 In the same way, you who are younger, submit yourselves to your elders. All of you, clothe yourselves with humility toward one another, because, "God opposes the proud but shows favor to the humble."

Your identity as a Man

Your identity is not found in power, money, or anything else. You are the son of God. That is your identity.

Galatians 3:26 For in Christ Jesus you are all sons of God, through faith.

Real Strength

Your strength is found in God

Joshua 1:9 Have I not commanded you? Be strong and courageous. Do not be afraid; do not be discouraged, for the LORD your God will be with you wherever you go.

Real men are humble

Arrogance is a disguise for insecurity. Real men are humble.

Luke 14:11 For all those who exalt themselves will be humbled, and those who humble themselves will be exalted.

On Purity

Purity comes from reading and doing God's word.

Psalms 119:9 How can a young person stay on the path of purity? By living according to your word.

Who are you trying to persuade

**Trying to 'keep up with the Joneses' is pointless.
Seek to please God.**

*Galatians 1:10 For do I now persuade men, or God?
or do I seek to please men? for if I yet pleased men,
I should not be the servant of Christ.*

Who do you surround yourself with

Build a community of Godly, Christian men. They will help you strengthen your faith.

Proverbs 27:17 As iron sharpens iron, so one person sharpens another.

Confess your sins

When you sin, confess to a trusted friend, or a mentor. This is the way to receive healing for any damage the sin may have caused.

James 5:16 Therefore confess your sins to each other and pray for each other so that you may be healed. The prayer of a righteous person is powerful and effective.

Resisting Temptation

The temptation may come in all forms, shapes, and sizes. But if you submit yourself to God, he will give you the strength to resist it.

James 4:7 7 Submit yourselves, then, to God. Resist the devil, and he will flee from you.

My sufficiency is of God.

(2 Corinthians 3:5 KJV): Not that we are sufficient of ourselves to think anything as of ourselves; but our sufficiency is of God;

I fear no evil, for the Lord is with me.

(Psalm 23:4 KJV): Yea, though I walk through the valley of the shadow of death, I will fear no evil: for thou art with me; thy rod and thy staff they comfort me.

My voice and my supplications are heard by God.

(Psalm 116:1-2 KJV):

(1) I love the LORD, because he hath heard my voice and my supplications.

(2) Because he hath inclined his ear unto me, therefore will I call upon him as long as I live.

I do not rely on my understanding but always acknowledge him for I know that he directs my path as it is written in

(Proverbs 3:5-6 KJV):

(5) Trust in the LORD with all thine heart; and lean not unto thine own understanding.

(6) In all thy ways acknowledge him, and he shall direct thy paths.

God is my helper

(Psalm 121:1-2 NLT):

(1) I look up to the mountains—does my help come from there?

(2) My help comes from the Lord,

 who made heaven and earth!

God makes me strong

(Psalm 138:3 NLT):

As soon as I pray, you answer me; you encourage me by giving me strength.

I am forgiven

(Ephesians 1:7 NLT):

He is so rich in kindness and grace that he purchased our freedom with the blood of his Son and forgave our sins.

I am chosen by God

(Ephesians 1:4 NLT):

Even before he made the world, God loved us and chose us in Christ to be holy and without fault in his eyes.

I trust God's timing

(Ecclesiastes 3:11 NLT):

Yet God has made everything beautiful for its own time. He has planted eternity in the human heart, but even so, people cannot see the whole scope of God's work from beginning to end.

God's mercy won't abandon me.

(Isaiah 54:10 NLT):

For the mountains may move and the hills disappear, but even then, my faithful love for you will remain. My covenant of blessing will never be broken," says the Lord, who has mercy on you.

My past will not define me

(Isaiah 43:18-19 NLT): (18) "But forget all that—it is nothing compared to what I am going to do.

(19) For I am about to do something new. See, I have already begun! Do you not see it? I will make a pathway through the wilderness. I will create rivers in the dry wasteland.

I can see beauty in everything

(Ecclesiastes 3:11 NLT): Yet God has made everything beautiful for its own time. He has planted eternity in the human heart, but even so, people cannot see the whole scope of God's work from beginning to end.

I'm sustained by the Lord

(Psalms 3:5 KJV): I laid me down and slept; I awaked; for the LORD sustained me.

I will trust the Lord because he is my refuge and fortress.

(Psalms 91:2 KJV): I will say of the LORD, He is my refuge and my fortress: my God; in him will I trust.

The mercy of God endureth forever for me, for I fear the Lord.

(Psalm 118:4 KJV): Let them now that fear the LORD say, that his mercy endureth for ever.

It is written, the Lord has delivered me from every noisome pestilence.

(Psalms 91:3 KJV): Surely he shall deliver thee from the snare of the fowler, and from the noisome pestilence.

The mercy of God endureth forever for me, for I fear the Lord

(Psalm 118:4 KJV): Let them now that fear the LORD say, that his mercy endureth for ever.

I will rejoice and be glad, for this is the day the Lord has made.

(Psalms 118:24 KJV): This is the day which the LORD hath made; we will rejoice and be glad in it.

I'm a good, firm, and honourable man, I stand with dignity.

(Isaiah 32:8 NLT): But generous people plan to do what is generous, and they stand firm in their generosity.

I am a modest man, caring, unselfish, giving, kind, and dependable.

(Ephesians 4:32 NLT): Instead, be kind to each other, tender hearted, forgiving one another, just as God through Christ has forgiven you.

I obey the Lord and live according to his will, I speak God's message in season and out of season.

(Deuteronomy 8:6 NLT): "So obey the commands of the Lord your God by walking in his ways and fearing him.

I am a giver, a guardian, a keeper, and a lover

(1 Timothy 5:8 NLT): But those who won't care for their relatives, especially those in their own household, have denied the true faith. Such people are worse than unbelievers.

I resist youthful lusts and I begin to live a pure life.

(Philippians 4:8 NLT): And now, dear brothers and sisters, one final thing. Fix your thoughts on what is true, and honorable, and right, and pure, and lovely, and admirable. Think about things that are excellent and worthy of praise.

I don't make room for sin, I don't tolerate adultery, uncleanness, or covetousness.

(Ephesians 4:26-27 KJV): (26)Be ye angry, and sin not: let not the sun go down upon your wrath:

(27) Neither give place to the devil.

I can do all things through Christ that strengthens me.

(Philippians 4:13 KJV): I can do all things through Christ which strengtheneth me.

The Lord is my light and my salvation

(Psalm 27:1 NIV): The Lord is my light and my salvation—so why should I be afraid? The Lord is my fortress, protecting me from danger, so why should I tremble?

The Lord is with me I shall not be afraid of what mere mortals can do to me.

(Psalm 118:6 NIV): The Lord is for me, so I will have no fear. What can mere people do to me?

For the spirit of the Lord does not make me timid but gives me power.

Timothy 1:7 NIV): For God has not given us a spirit of fear and timidity, but of power, love, and self-discipline.

I'm God's workmanship

(Ephesians 2:10 KJV):

For we are his workmanship, created in Christ Jesus unto good works, which God hath before ordained that we should walk in them.

I'm bold as a lion

(Proverbs 28:1 KJV): The wicked flee when no man pursueth: but the righteous are bold as a lion.

I'm fearless, the Lord is the strength of my life

(Psalm 27:1 KJV): The LORD is my light and my salvation; whom shall I fear? the LORD is the strength of my life; of whom shall I be afraid?

I make the right decisions, and I am prepared for a wonderful and rewarding future.

(Jeremiah 29:11 NIV): For I know the plans I have for you," declares the Lord, "plans to prosper you and not to harm you, plans to give you hope and a future.

I am seeking the kingdom of my father, God, and his righteousness first.

(Matthew 6:33 KJV): But seek ye first the kingdom of God, and his righteousness; and all these things shall be added unto you.

the lines have fallen unto me in pleasant places.

(Psalm 16:6 NIV): The boundary lines have fallen for me in pleasant places; surely I have a delightful inheritance.

I am exalting and loving the Lord with all my heart, mind, and soul.

(Mark 12:30 NIV): Love the Lord your God with all your heart and with all your soul and with all your mind and with all your strength.

I'm strong and courageous, I'm not afraid, I'm not discouraged for the Lord my God is always with me.

(Deuteronomy 31:6 NIV): Be strong and courageous. Do not be afraid or terrified because of them, for the Lord your God goes with you; he will never leave you nor forsake you."

I'm blessed because the Lord fulfills his promises to me.

(Luke 1:45 KJV): And blessed is she that believed: for there shall be a performance of those things which were told her from the Lord.

I am clothed with strength and dignity

(Proverbs 31:25 KJV): Strength and honour are her clothing; and she shall rejoice in time to come.

I am a man who has made a covenant with God, I choose to love and follow Him, and I cling to Him in all I do; this is my life.

(Deuteronomy 30:20 KJV): That thou mayest love the LORD thy God, and that thou mayest obey his voice, and that thou mayest cleave unto him: for he is thy life, and the length of thy days: that thou mayest dwell in the land which the LORD sware unto thy fathers, to Abraham, to Isaac, and to Jacob, to give them.

Every curse operating in my life is nailed with Jesus on the Cross of Calvary.

(Galatians 3:13 NIV): Christ redeemed us from the curse of the law by becoming a curse for us, for it is written: "Cursed is everyone who is hung on a pole."

I am exalting and loving the Lord with all my heart, mind, and soul.

(Mark 12:30 KJV): And thou shalt love the Lord thy God with all thy heart, and with all thy soul, and with all thy mind, and with all thy strength: this is the first commandment.

I am always looking to the Lord for strength. I seek him always.

(1 chronicle 16:11 KJV): Seek the LORD and his strength, seek his face continually.

I am justified by faith, and I have peace with God through my savior, Jesus Christ.

(Romans 5:1 KJV): Therefore being justified by faith, we have peace with God through our Lord Jesus Christ.

The works of my hand are blessed

(Deuteronomy 28:12 NIV): The Lord will open the heavens, the storehouse of his bounty, to send rain on your land in season and to bless all the work of your hands. You will lend to many nations but will borrow from none.

I am a blessing to my Generation and the Nation; Nations shall call me blessed of the Lord.

(Malachi 3:12 NIV): "Then all the nations will call you blessed, for yours will be a delightful land," says the Lord Almighty.

No enchantment or divination against me shall stand.

(Numbers 23:23 KJV): Surely there is no enchantment against Jacob, neither is there any divination against Israel: according to this time it shall be said of Jacob and of Israel, What hath God wrought!

Jesus has bought me with his blood therefore I belong to Jesus.

(I Corinthians 6:20 NIV): you were bought at a price. Therefore honor God with your bodies.

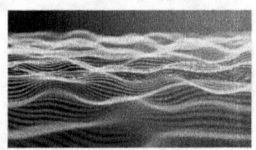

I'm fearfully and wonderfully made, and I praise the Lord

(Psalm 139:14 NIV): I praise you because I am fearfully and wonderfully made; your works are wonderful, I know that full well.

It is written, I'm the Son of God because the Spirit of God lives inside of me.

(Romans 8:6 NIV): The mind governed by the flesh is death, but the mind governed by the Spirit is life and peace.

My Father is the Lion of the tribe of Judah

**(Revelation 5:5 NIV): Then one of the elders said
to me, "Do not weep! See, the Lion of the tribe of
Judah, the Root of David, has triumphed. He is able
to open the scroll and its seven seals."**

No weapon designed against me or my job will prosper.

(Isaiah 54:17 NIV):

no weapon forged against you will prevail, and you will refute every tongue that accuses you. This is the heritage of the servants of the Lord, and this is their vindication from me," declares the Lord.

Listen

God's righteousness does not mix with man's anger. It is like oil and water. In heated and emotional conversations, your top priority as a godly man is to listen.

James 1:19-20 Wherefore, my beloved brethren, let every man be swift to hear, slow to speak, slow to wrath: For the wrath of man worketh not the righteousness of God.

Seek God

Let seeking God be your top priority over seeking wealth, romance, power, or anything else. Everything else will come in due time.

Matthew 6:33 But seek first the kingdom of God and his righteousness, and all these things will be added to you.

Being a Godly Father

Let your children see God in you. Discipline them with love.

Ephesians 6:4 Fathers, do not provoke your children to anger, but bring them up in the discipline and instruction of the Lord.

Goals and callings

Forget past mistakes. Focus on the goals ahead.

Philippians 3:13-14 Brethren, I count not myself to have apprehended: but this one thing I do, forgetting those things which are behind, and reaching forth unto those things which are before, I press toward the mark for the prize of the high calling of God in Christ Jesus

Be a man of Integrity

Integrity is the mark of a righteous man. So do the right thing always. Even and especially when no one is looking.

Proverbs 20:7 The righteous who walks in his integrity— blessed are his children after him!

Being a Godly Husband

Whether your wife is in the future or the present. You are called to love her deeply and truly.

Ephesians 5:25 Husbands, love your wives, just as Christ loved the church and gave himself up for her.

How God disciplines us

When facing God's discipline through the consequences of your actions. Always remember that he is a good father, and he loves you. That is why he disciplines you.

Proverbs 3:11-12 My son, do not despise the LORD's discipline or be weary of his reproof, for the LORD reproves him whom he loves, as a father the son in whom he delights.

Meditate on God's Word

Meditate on God's word. Keep it close to your heart and practice it. This is how you will find peace.

Proverbs 3:1 My son, do not forget my law, But let your heart keep my commands;
For length of days and long life
And peace they will add to you.

Hold on to your faith

Hold on to your faith and what you believe. Do not let yourself be corrupted by the things of the world.

1 Corinthians 16:13 Be watchful, stand firm in the faith, act like men, be strong.

Treat your wife with kindness

Your prayer life and relationship with God is directly affected by how you treat those closest to you. So, treat them with kindness, and your prayers will not be hindered.

1 Peter 3:7 In the same way, you husbands must give honor to your wives. Treat your wife with understanding as you live together. She may be weaker than you are, but she is your equal partner in God's gift of new life. Treat her as you should so your prayers will not be hindered

When in doubt, ask. When in need, ask

You do not have to figure everything out on your own. You've got God. A loving father who is willing to help you and give you what you need every step of the way.

Matthew 7:7 Ask, and it will be given to you; seek, and you will find; knock, and it will be opened to you.

Wisdom and discretion with women

Use discretion in the company you keep, especially when it comes to women. Listen to God and you will not be ensnared.

Proverbs 5:1-3 My son, pay attention to my wisdom, turn your ear to my words of insight, that you may maintain discretion and your lips may preserve knowledge. For the lips of the adulterous woman drip honey, and her speech is smoother than oil;

God's grace

God is not afraid of your sin. No matter how far you have strayed and how much you have messed up. He can make you clean.

*Isaiah 1:18 "Come now, let us reason together, says the L*ORD*: though your sins are like scarlet, they shall be as white as snow; though they are red like crimson, they shall become like wool.*

Growth

Look at your life closely. Have you changed? Have you grown? Maybe it is time to put away childish things.

1 Corinthians 13:11 When I was a child, I spoke like a child, I thought like a child, I reasoned like a child. When I became a man, I gave up childish ways.

Feed your spirit

You are not made to survive on physical food alone, but also on spiritual food.

Matthew 4:4 But he answered, "It is written, 'Man shall not live by bread alone, but by every word that comes from the mouth of God.'"

Be a good example

It is often said that 'You may be the only Bible that some people read.' Set a good example and always remember whom you represent.

Titus 2:7 Show yourself in all respects to be a model of good works, and in your teaching show integrity, dignity,

Put God's will before Your plans

Do not be so set in your ways or rigid about what should happen and how it should happen. Always recognize that God's will reigns supreme.

Proverbs 16:9 The heart of man plans his way, but the LORD establishes his steps.

Work hard and hone your skills.

God gives you time to grow in your talents and skills, use that time wisely because, in due course, He will bring you to the right place and before the right people.

Proverbs 22:29 Do you see a man who excels in his work? He will stand before kings; He will not stand before unknown men.

A living sacrifices

Deny yourselves the evil desires of your heart. This is how you offer yourself as a living sacrifice to God.

Romans 12:1 I appeal to you therefore, brothers by the mercies of God, to present your bodies as a living sacrifice, holy and acceptable to God, which is your spiritual worship

The power of your tongue

Your words are more powerful than you can imagine and can hurt and injure just like any physical weapon. Use them to build, not to destroy.

James 3:7-9 For every kind of beast and bird, of reptile and sea creature, can be tamed and has been tamed by mankind, but no human being can tame the tongue. It is a restless evil, full of deadly poison. With it we bless our Lord and Father, and with it we curse people who are made in the likeness of God.

Don't be jealous of the wicked

If you see other men who seem to be blessed and get ahead from cheating or being wicked, stand firm in your integrity and honor. They will get what they deserve.

Psalm 37:1-2 Fret not yourself because of evildoers; be not envious of wrongdoers! For they will soon fade like the grass and wither like the green herb.

Depend on God

Do not depend on yourself. Depend on God.

Jeremiah 17:5 Thus says the LORD:
"Cursed is the man who trusts in man and makes flesh
his strength, whose heart turns away from the LORD."

God > Fear

Whatever you may be facing, in your finances, relationships, or even health. You do not need to be afraid. You only need to trust in God.

Proverbs 29:25 The fear of man lays a snare, but whoever trusts in the LORD is safe.

Let your yes be a yes and your no be a no

When you speak, there is no need to make lofty promises or swear to convince someone of the integrity of your word. As a Godly man, speak candidly and honestly, that is all that is needed.

James 5:12 But above all, my brothers, do not swear, either by heaven or by earth or by any other oath, but let your "yes" be yes and your "no" be no, so that you may not fall under condemnation.

Equip yourself to be a man of God

God's word is the only tool you need and the only tool that can equip you to be a true man of God.

2 Timothy 3:16-17 All Scripture is breathed out by God and profitable for teaching, for reproof, for correction, and for training in righteousness, that the man of God may be complete, equipped for every good work.

Amazing Grace

This is the gospel. This is amazing grace. That Jesus loved you so much that he gave up his own life. So never believe that you are alone, unloved, worthless, or useless. You are worth the blood of Jesus.

John 15:13 Greater love hath no man than this, that a man lay down his life for his friends.

If this book has blessed you, please take the time to write a review on Amazon and Barnes and Noble, or wherever you have purchased this book. Share this book with your friends, prayer groups, churches, and on all platforms to build and strengthen men.

Thank you, for your support!

We would love to hear from you, email us at

rightsideceo@yahoo.com

for publishing visit the website below

www.rightsidepublishing.com

Notes

_____

_____

_____

_____

_____

_____

_____

_____

_____

_____

_____

_____

_____

Notes